The Great Instrumentalists
IN HISTORIC PHOTOGRAPHS

The Great Instrumentalists
IN HISTORIC PHOTOGRAPHS
274 Portraits from 1850 to 1950

Edited by
JAMES CAMNER

Dover Publications, Inc.
New York

PICTURE CREDITS

Editor and publisher are grateful to the following lenders of photographs:

Angel Records: 27.
Gregor Benko: 5, 20, 26, 43, 45, 52, 60, 75, 139, 140, 152, 163, 168, 176, 178, 225, 226, 248, 264.
Suzanne Bloch: 8, 11, 22, 69.
Norman Crider (Ballet Shop): 112, 114, 190.
Detroit Symphony: 169.
EMI Records: 81, 88, 133, 213, 220, 238, 252.
Arthur Forman: 151.
Joseph Gold: 2, 62, 262.
International Piano Archives: 61, 89, 131.
Rudolf Kallir: 31, 124, 236.
Lim Lai: 1, 3, 6, 28, 30, 50, 57, 67, 70, 71, 72, 76, 77, 83, 93, 97, 98, 100, 101, 104, 106, 116, 123, 126, 128, 136, 137, 138, 141, 143, 144, 145, 148, 159, 180, 184, 205, 207, 214, 215, 216, 219, 230, 232, 233, 242, 254, 258, 262.
Janet Lehr: 111.
Philadelphia Orchestra: 135.
Oscar Shapiro: 29, 33, 36, 59, 103, 117, 179, 185, 193, 195, 235, 269, 272.
Anna Sosenko (Autographs): 44, 66, 102, 142, 155, 187, 211.
Robert Tuggle: 9, 12, 14, 15, 17, 24, 34, 35, 37, 41, 42, 47, 48, 53, 54, 55, 56, 63, 82, 85, 87, 90, 91, 94, 96, 99, 105, 108, 109, 110, 113, 115, 121, 122, 125, 127, 129, 130, 134, 149, 153, 154, 158, 165, 167, 172, 175, 177, 189, 191, 194, 196, 197, 200, 201, 202, 204, 209, 210, 217, 222, 223, 224, 231, 237, 243, 244, 250, 257, 263, 265, 266, 267, 271, 274.

Published in Canada by General Publishing Company, Ltd., 30 Lesmill Road, Don Mills, Toronto, Ontario.
Published in the United Kingdom by Constable and Company, Ltd., 10 Orange Street, London WC2H 7EG.

The Great Instrumentalists in Historic Photographs is a new work, first published by Dover Publications, Inc., in 1980.

International Standard Book Number: 0-486-23907-1
Library of Congress Catalog Card Number: 79-93249

Manufactured in the United States of America
Dover Publications, Inc.
180 Varick Street
New York, N.Y. 10014

INTRODUCTION

In their day, the popularity of a Liszt, Paderewski, Sarasate or Anton Rubinstein was unrivaled by even that of a Jenny Lind or Sarah Bernhardt. Throughout the nineteenth and early twentieth centuries the great instrumentalists were treated to hysterical demonstrations of affection usually accorded today only to pop singers. Many of the greatest appeared on the scene too early to make recordings, but were captured by the camera, which preceded the phonograph by roughly half a century. To have these photographs is no small consolation. (What wouldn't we give for one of Bach or Mozart?) In them we can see the handsome romanticism of Liszt, the wild, "echt"-virtuoso look of Ysaÿe, the commanding gaze of the women virtuosos, Eibenschütz, Ney, Neruda.

Along with most of the great fiddlers and pianists of the photographic era, we are pleased to have a generous representation of organists, flutists, lutenists, even double-bass players. All the portraits are interesting, but our favorites perhaps are those of the child prodigies, often photographed in sailor suits. Not all of the gifted children look happy in these photos; some were, unknowingly, already at the peak of their careers.

Photos of instrumentalists were avidly collected from the very beginning of photography. Remarkably, as early as the turn of the century a forgery was widely circulated, the Paganini photograph faked by two men in the 1890s. They claimed to have found a daguerreotype of that most legendary of all the virtuosos, and even convinced the distinguished firm of Breitkopf & Härtel of its authenticity. That firm published a gravure from it which is still in circulation and has even been reproduced as genuine in some books. We reproduce it here as a fascinating relic and quite obviously a forgery to modern eyes. (Paganini was contacted by a photographer shortly before his death, but was too ill to make an appointment and, as far as we know, there are no photographs of the great man.)

The time span covered by the present volume ends with the period immediately following World War II,

The notorious fake photograph of Paganini.

which coincides, sadly, with the premature deaths of some of the most promising new talents: Dennis Brain, Dinu Lipatti, Ginette Neveu and William Kapell. The pictures are arranged in a single alphabetical order, and the performers are indexed by their instruments.

We wish to thank all the generous contributors who made this book possible (see the list of picture credits), with special thanks to Lim Lai and Gregor Benko for their knowledgeable assistance.

JAMES CAMNER

The Great Instrumentalists
IN HISTORIC PHOTOGRAPHS

1

2

1. EUGÈNE D'ALBERT (1864–1932), German pianist and composer, born in Scotland. One of Liszt's greatest pupils; renowned for his playing of Beethoven. Teresa Carreño was his first wife. (Photo: H. Lessmann, Munich)

2. ALFREDO D'AMBROSIO (1871–1914), Italian violinist. A pupil of Sarasate and Wilhelmj, he led a famous string quartet in Nice. (Photo: Henri Manuel, Paris; signed Paris, 1913)

3

4

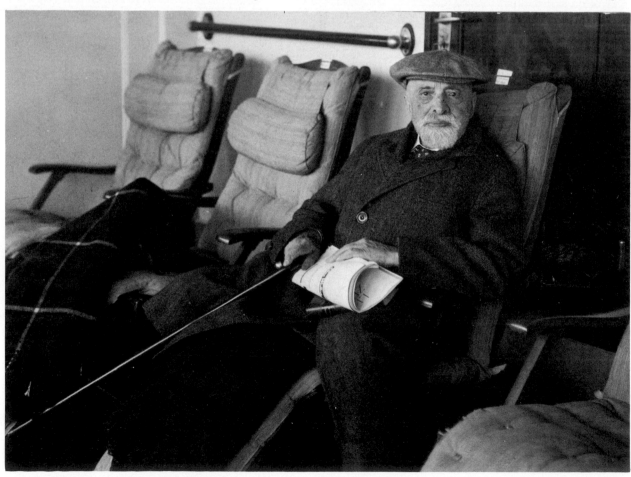

2

5

6

7

3. CONRAD ANSORGE (1862–1930), German pianist. One of Liszt's last pupils, he was known as a "metaphysician among pianists" for his Beethoven, Schubert and Schumann. He toured America and Russia. 4. CLAUDIO ARRAU (born 1903), Chilean pianist. He made his American debut in 1923; one of the legendary pianists still active. (Photo signed 1941) 5. LEOPOLD AUER (1845–1930), Hungarian violinist and teacher. Student of Joachim; went to Russia to perform in the Imperial Orchestra and teach at the conservatory. His pupils included Elman, Zimbalist and Heifetz. 6 & 7. WILHELM BACKHAUS (1884–1969), German pianist. Pupil of Reckendorf and d'Albert. Internationally acclaimed, especially for his Beethoven, he toured the U.S. in 1912–1914, 1954 and 1956. (Photo 6: Ellis & Wallery)

8

9

10

4

11

Issay Barmas.

12

8. LOUIS BAILLY (born 1882), French-American violist (shown standing between the composer Ernst Bloch and the pianist Harold Bauer). Bailly was a member of the Flonzaley and Curtis Quartets and was head of the viola and chamber music departments at the Curtis Institute of Music in Philadelphia. (Photo taken in the Berkshires, 1919) 9. OTTO BARBLAN (1860–1943), Swiss organist and composer. Associated with the Cathedral of Geneva. (Photo: A. de Lalancy, Geneva) 10. SIMON BARER (1896–1951), Russian pianist. Pupil of Anna Essipoff; winner of the Rubinstein Prize. He died during a concert in Carnegie Hall. (Photo: Maurice Seymour, Chicago) 11. ALEXANDER BARJANSKY, cellist. It was for him that Ernst Bloch wrote *Schelomo*. (Photo: Ernst Bloch) 12. ISSAY BARMAS (1872–1946), Russian violinist and teacher. A student of Joachim, he toured Europe and settled in London. (Photo: E. Bieber, Berlin; signed Berlin, 1909)

13

14

15

16

17

13. GEORGE BARRÈRE (1876–1944), French flutist (shown with his Little Symphony). Considered the outstanding flutist of his time, he came to America in 1905 and played in the N.Y. Symphony Orchestra until 1928. See also photo 143. (Photo signed Akron, 1929) 14. HEINRICH BARTH (1847–1922), German pianist. Pupil of von Bülow and Tausig. Founded the Barth Trio with the violinist Heinrich De Ahna and the cellist Robert Hausmann. (Photo: Oscar Brettschneider; signed Berlin, 1909) 15. RICHARD BARTH (1850–1923), German vio-linist. Student of Joachim; famed for his left-handed bow technique. (Photo: Atelier Moosigay, Hamburg, 1908; signed Hamburg, 1909) 16. HAROLD BAUER (1873–1951), British-German pianist. Began as a violinist, then studied piano with Paderewski. Made his American debut in 1900 with the Boston Symphony. (Photo: Apeda, N.Y.) 17. FELIX BERBER (1871–1930), Austrian violinist active in Germany. A student of Brodsky, he was acclaimed in his tour of the U. S. in 1910. (Photo: A. de Lalancy, Geneva, ca. 1908; signed Geneva, 1909)

18

19

20

21

18. CHARLES-WILFRIDE DE BÉRIOT (1883–1914), French pianist. Son of Charles-Auguste de Bériot, famed Belgian violinist. A pupil of Thalberg, he taught piano at the Paris Conservatoire. (Photo: Antony, Paris; signed 1901) 19 & 20. LAZAR BERMAN (born 1930), Russian pianist. Legendary in Russia, especially for his titanic playing of Liszt, he was virtually unknown in the West until his sensational American tour in 1976. (Photos ca. 1950 and 1976, respectively) 21. EDWARD POWER BIGGS (1906–1977), British-American organist. He became renowned in the U. S. through radio recitals. (Photo: Bachrach, N.Y.)

22. SUZANNE BLOCH (born 1907), Swiss-born lutenist and harpsichordist. Daughter and student of Ernst Bloch; also studied with Nadia Boulanger. The first famous lutenist of modern times, and a pioneer in twentieth-century performances of polyphonic music on old and original instruments.
23. GIOVANNI BOTTESINI (1821–1889), Italian double-bass virtuoso, conductor and composer. The outstanding nineteenth-century performer on his instrument, he toured worldwide, also playing solo cello. He conducted the world premiere of *Aïda* in Cairo in 1871.

24

25

24. JOHANNES BRAHMS (1833–1897), German composer and pianist. The master composer was a famous child prodigy and gave a celebrated piano recital in Hamburg at age fourteen. He later was the soloist in the first performance of his great second piano concerto. (Photo: Adèle, Vienna, 1873) 25. ALEXANDER BRAILOWSKY (born 1896), Russian pianist. Specialist in Chopin. (Photo: Halsman, Paris; signed 1939) 26. JORGE BOLET (born 1914), Cuban pianist. Renowned for his playing of Liszt. 27. DENNIS BRAIN (1921–1957), English virtuoso on the French horn. A member of a famous English family of French horn players, he studied with his father Aubrey and became the most celebrated performer on his instrument in history. (Photo: George Maiteny, London)

26

28

14

29

30

31

28. JULIAN BREAM (born 1933), English guitar and lute virtuoso. 29. BRODSKY QUARTETTE. The second of the two famous quartets founded by the legendary Russian violinist Adolf Brodsky (1851–1929), to whom Tchaikovsky dedicated his violin concerto. Left to right: S. Spielman, C. Fuchs, Brodsky, Bowden-Briggs. (Photo: Percy Guttenberg, Manchester) 30. ANTON BRUCKNER (1824–1896), Austrian composer and organist. Most celebrated in his lifetime as an organist, he established his reputation on his tours of France in 1869 and England in 1871. (Photo: A. Huber, Vienna) 31. IGNAZ BRÜLL (1846–1907), Austrian pianist and composer. A close friend of Brahms, Brüll made extensive recital tours before pursuing a career as an opera composer. (Photo: F. Luckhardt, Vienna)

32

32. BUDAPEST QUARTET. The most celebrated string quartet of the century was founded in Budapest in 1921. The members pictured in this composite photo are not the originals, but were the principals when the group was enjoying its greatest fame. Left to right: Josef Roisman (1st violin), Alexander Schneider (2nd violin), Boris Kroyt (viola), Mischa Schneider (cello). (Photo 1933; signed 1938) 33 & 34. OLE BULL (1810–1880), Norwegian violinist. Of great fame in the U. S. in the nineteenth century, he is seen in photo 34 (by Rocher, Chicago) seated beside the American soprano Emma Thursby, with whom he toured.

33

35

36

18

37

38

35. HANS VON BÜLOW (1830–1894), German pianist and conductor. A student of Friedrich Wieck and of Liszt, he was renowned for his performances of Beethoven. As a conductor he was associated with Wagner and led the world premiere of *Tristan und Isolde* in 1865. (Photo: J. Stuky, Neuchâtel) 36. WILLY BURMESTER (1869–1933), German violinist. Pupil of Joachim; a popular virtuoso who made frequent concert tours of the U. S. and Europe beginning in 1886. (Photo: Otto Becker & Maass, Berlin) 37. ADOLF BUSCH (1891–1952), German violinist. Founder of the famed Busch Quartet and Busch Trio. (Photo: Theo Schafgans, Bonn) 38. FERRUCCIO BUSONI (1866–1924), Italian pianist and composer active in Germany. One of the first of the modern intellectual pianists, Busoni was one of the giants of his time. He cultivated a large repertory that included Bach, Beethoven and Liszt.

39

41

40

39 & 40. ROBERT CASADESUS (1899–1972), French pianist. A member of a famous musical family, Casadesus was an internationally known pianist. (Photo 39: Wulffing, Paris; signed 1935. Photo 40: Halsman, N.Y.; signed 1947) 41 & 42. (MARÍA) TERESA CARREÑO (1853–1917), Venezuelan pianist. A sensational child prodigy, she gave a recital at Irving Hall in New York at age eight (photo 41). Later she studied with Gottschalk and Rubinstein and, after an interlude as an opera soprano, established herself as one of the great pianists of her time. Her four husbands included Emile Sauret and Eugène d'Albert. (Photo 42: J. Gurney & Son, N.Y.)

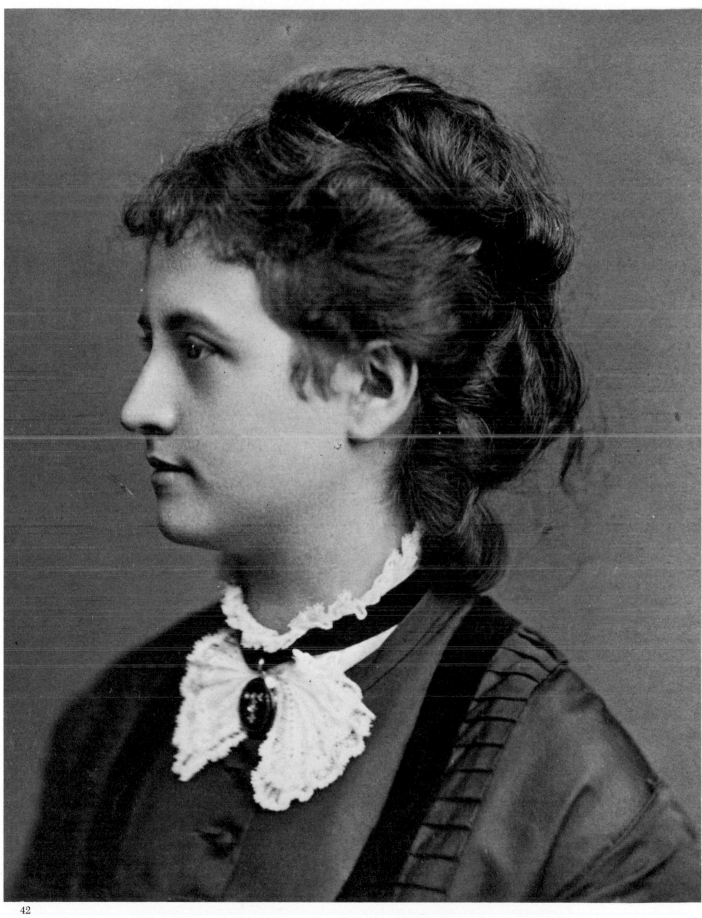

42

43

43. GEORGE COPELAND (1882–1971), American pianist. Student of Buonamici; famed as an interpreter of Debussy, whose friend he was and much of whose music he introduced to America. 44. PABLO CASALS (1876–1973), Spanish cellist. One of the most idolized musicians of the twentieth century, his name was synonymous with the cello. He formed a famous trio with Thibaud and Cortot and founded festivals at Prades and in Puerto Rico. See also photo 46.

45

46

47

45. JEANNE-MARIE DARRÉ (born 1905), French pianist. 46. ALFRED CORTOT (1877–1962), Swiss pianist. Seen here as one of the famous trio that included the cellist Pablo Casals (see photo 44) and the violinist Jacques Thibaud (see photo 255). 47. FERDINAND DAVID (1810–1873), German violinist and teacher. A pupil of Spohr and Hauptmann, he became first violinist of the Leipzig Gewandhaus Orchestra in 1836 at Mendelssohn's request. He advised Mendelssohn during the composition of the violin concerto and played the world premiere in 1845. His pupils included Joachim and Wilhelmj. (Photo: August Brasch, Leipzig)

DIÉMER

48

48. LOUIS DIÉMER (1843–1919), French pianist. A pupil of Marmontel, he specialized in recitals of old music and established the Société des Anciens Instruments. Saint-Saëns and Lalo wrote music for him. (Photo: Gautin Fils, Paris; signed 1909) 49. FANNY DAVIES (1861–1934), English pianist. Pupil of Reinecke and Clara Schumann; her career took her to Germany, France and Italy. 50. MAURICIO DENGREMONT (1866–1893), Brazilian violinist. He became famous as a child prodigy during a European tour in 1877. (Photo: Anderson, N.Y.)

49

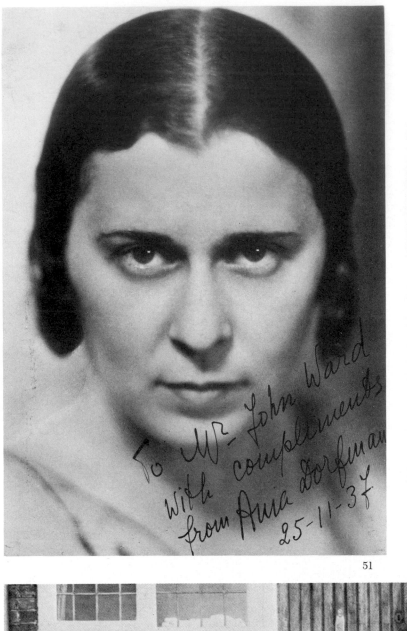

To Mr. John Ward with compliments from Ania Dorfman 25-11-37

Ernst v. Dohnányi

51

53

28

52

54

51. ANIA DORFMANN (born 1899), Russian pianist. Pupil of Isidor Philipp. Her career led to an appearance and recording with Toscanini and the NBC Symphony. (Photo signed 1937) 52. ARNOLD DOLMETSCH (1858–1940), English instrumentalist and music antiquarian (born in France). He was chiefly responsible for the revival of interest in old music and instruments, many of which he restored and built. In the photo (a family consort of viols) he is third from the left; the others, left to right, being his children Rudolph, Cecile, Nathalie and Carl, and his wife Mabel. Carl, a great recorder virtuoso, manages Arnold Dolmetsch, Ltd., Musical Instrument Makers. (Photo ca. 1929) 53 & 54. ERNST VON DOHNÁNYI (1877–1960), Hungarian pianist, conductor and composer. His first piano recital in 1897 established him as an artist of the first rank. Brahms, as an old man, admired his early music. (Photo 54: Abresch, N.Y.; signed 1948)

55

56

55. ALEXANDER DREYSCHOCK (1818–1869), Bohemian pianist. Of legendary virtuosity, he was considered a rival of Liszt. (Photo: Hugo Danz, Berlin) 56. RAIMUND DREYSCHOCK (1824–1869), Bohemian violinist, brother of Alexander. Raimund was concertmaster of the famed Gewandhaus concerts in Leipzig and a professor of violin at the conservatory there. (Photo: Hugo Danz, Berlin) 57. MARCEL DUPRÉ (1886–1970), French organist. A pupil of Widor and perhaps the outstanding organist of his time, he toured worldwide beginning in 1921. (Photo: Underwood & Underwood) 58. MAURICE EISENBERG (1900–1972), German-American cellist. Student of Becker, Klengel and Casals; first cellist with the Philadelphia Orchestra (1917–19), he also had a career as a soloist. (Photo: Lipnitzki, Paris, ca. 1933)

57

58

59

60

59 & 60. MISCHA ELMAN (1891–1967), Russian violinist. Student of Leopold Auer and an extraordinary prodigy, he was considered a premier violinist at his debut in 1904. His first triumphal tour of the U. S. was in 1908. (Photo 60: Alban, Paris; inscribed 1929 to Josef Hofmann) 61. ILONA EIBENSCHÜTZ (1873–1967), Hungarian pianist. Pupil of Clara Schumann. A great prodigy, she became a favorite pianist of Brahms and gave the world premiere of many of his piano works at his request. She formed a trio with Piatti and Joachim in London. Her career was short as she retired after her early marriage.

62

64

63

65

66

62 & 63. HEINRICH WILHELM ERNST (1814–1865), Moravian violinist and composer. This famous virtuoso made his first successful tour at the age of sixteen. (Photo 63: H. Lenthall, London) 64. GEORGES ENESCO (1881–1955), Rumanian composer and violinist. Student of Fauré and Massenet. His career took him all over the world as a violinist and conductor. A village was named after him in Rumania. His most celebrated pupil was Yehudi Menuhin. See also photo 144. (Photo: Rauhoff-Richter, Chicago) 65. EMANUEL FEUERMANN (1902–1942), Galician cellist. Student of Walter and Klengel. Considered by some to be superior to Casals, Feuermann made his U. S. debut with the N.Y. Philharmonic in 1935. (Photo signed 1935) 66. CARL FLESCH (1873–1944), Hungarian violinist. Equally famous as a teacher, he was active in the U. S. and Germany. (Photo signed 1928)

67

68

67. EDWIN FISCHER (1886–1960), Swiss pianist. Especially noted for his playing of Mozart. (Photo: A. Rohwer, Kiel) 68. RUDOLF FIRKUŠNÝ (born 1912), Czech pianist. Of individual temperament, he made his debut in Prague in 1922. (Photo signed 1952) 69. FLONZALEY QUARTET. String quartet founded by Edward J. de Coppet of New York in 1902. At the time of this photo, the members were Adolfo Betti, 1st violin; Alfred Pochon, 2nd violin; Louis Bailly, viola (see photo 8); and Iwan d'Archambeau, cello. The first great international quartet, it also encouraged new composers, including Ernst Bloch (shown standing). (Photo: Apeda, N.Y., 1918) 70. PIERRE FOURNIER (born 1906), French cellist. He often performed chamber music with Szigeti, Primrose and Schnabel, and had a successful solo career as well. (Photo: DG/Jacoby) 71. ARNOLD FOLDESY (born 1882), Hungarian cellist. Student of Popper. Toured the U. S. in 1917. (Photo: Lafayette, London)

69

70

71

72

73

72. CÉSAR FRANCK (1822–1890), Belgian composer and organist. As a child prodigy he gave piano recitals in Belgium. As organist at Sainte-Clotilde in Paris, his pupils included d'Indy, Duparc, Chausson and Pierné. (Photo: Pierre Petit) 73. MALCOLM FRAGER (born 1935), American pianist. His tours have included Russia and Iceland. (Photo: Abresch, N.Y.) 74. ZINO FRANCESCATTI (born 1902), French violinist. He made his debut at age five. See also photo 144. (Photo signed 1966)

74

75

77

76

78

75. IGNAZ FRIEDMAN (1882–1948), Polish pianist. Student of Leschetizky; considered one of the great pianists of his day; especially noted for his playing of Chopin; edited an edition of Chopin's works. 76. JOSEPH FUCHS (born 1900), American violinist. From 1926 to 1940, concertmaster of the Cleveland Orchestra. As a soloist he appeared with most of the major American and European orchestras. 77 & 78. OSSIP GABRILOVITCH (1878–1936), Russian-American pianist and conductor. A student of Rubinstein and Leschetizky, he began his career as a virtuoso in 1896 and made his successful first tour of America in 1900. After 1918 he was conductor of the Detroit Symphony but continued his piano career. (Photo 77: E. Bieber, Berlin)

79

79. RUDOLPH GANZ (1877–1972), Swiss-American pianist. A great figure
in American musical life, Ganz was almost as proficient on the cello.
80. RAYA GARBOUSOVA (born 1906), Russian cellist. Her career began in
1923 in Moscow; U. S. debut in 1934. (Photo: Dis, Paris; signed 1938)

81

81. EMIL GILELS (born 1916), Russian pianist. He first appeared in the West in Vienna in 1933. Since World War II he has been considered in the first rank of pianists. (Photo: Capitol Records Photographic Studio, Hollywood) 82. FRIEDRICH GERNSHEIM (1839–1916), German pianist, composer and conductor. Student of Rosenhain and Moscheles; he appeared as a boy pianist in Frank-furt. (Photo: Albert Meyer Nachf. Oscar Brettschneider; dated Berlin, 1904) 83 & 84. WALTER GIESEKING (1895–1956), German pianist born in France. Especially famous for his mastery of textures and gradations. (Photo 83: 1954. Photo 84: Nickolas Muray, 1927; signed N.Y., 1929)

83

82

84

85

86

87

88

89

85. ALEXANDER WILHELM GOTTSCHALG (1827–1908), German organist. Court organist at Weimar from 1870; associated with Liszt. (Photo: August Brasch, Leipzig) 86. ARABELLA GODDARD (1836–1922), English pianist born in France. Student of Kalkbrenner. Her international career took her to Germany, Italy, India and the U. S. (Photo: H. N. King, Bath) 87. LOUIS MOREAU GOTTSCHALK (1829–1869), American pianist and composer. Studied in Paris under Hallé. One of the leading pianists of his day, his concerts and tours were tremendous commercial successes. (Photo: Charles D. Fredricks & Co., N.Y.) 88. LEON GOOSSENS (born 1897), English oboist. Member of a famous musical family, he was a leading player at seventeen. 89 & 90. LEOPOLD GODOWSKY (1870–1938), Russian pianist. Protégé of Saint-Saëns; became an American citizen in 1891. Considered one of the most phenomenal technicians in pianistic history. His own compositions are considered almost unplayable because of their difficulty. (Photo 89: Fayer, Vienna. Photo 90: Alexander Eddy, N.Y.)

90

Cordial greetings
M. W. Lefevre
from

Franz
Bonn 191?

91

92

94

93

91. PERCY ALDRIDGE GRAINGER (1882–1961), Australian pianist and composer, naturalized American. He is especially remembered for his association with Grieg, who preferred his playing to that of all others. An original in his concertizing and composing, he was respected for his enormous and varied abilities. (Photo: Morse; signed 1927) 92. MARCEL GRANDJANY (1891–1975), French harpist. One of the few to achieve great fame on the harp, he made his U. S. debut in 1924. (Photo: Annie Friedberg, N.Y.; signed Quebec, 1948)   93. ARTHUR DE GREEF (1862–1940), Belgian pianist and composer. Toured Europe extensively. (Photo: Elliott & Fry)   94. EDVARD GRIEG (1843–1907), Norwegian composer and pianist. Studied piano with Plaidy and Moscheles. He played the solo part of his great piano concerto in 1869 at the age of twenty-five, becoming world famous as a composer and pianist. (Photo: Georg Brokesch, Leipzig, 1881; signed Bergen, 1881)

95

95. GRILLER STRING QUARTET. This distinguished quartet, founded by Sidney Griller (English violinist, born 1911), also included Jack O'Brien (2nd violin), Philip Burton (viola) and Colin Hampton (cello). 96. HEINRICH GRÜNFELD (1855–1931), Czech cellist. Distinguished as a soloist and as a chamber player with Scharwenka and Holländer. 97. CARL HALIR (1859–1909), Bohemian violinist. Pupil of Joachim. An original member of the Joachim Quartet (see photo 128), he later founded his own quartet. A tour of the U.S. in 1896 was very successful. 98. PAUL GRÜMMER (1879–1965), German cellist. Member of the Kubelík Quartet, then of the Busch Quartet. First cello of the Vienna Konzertverein. (Photo: Hughes & Mullins)

96

98

97

99

101

100

102

103

99. SIR CHARLES HALLÉ (1819–1895), German-British pianist and conductor. A prodigy, he concertized at age four. He gave concerts in 1846 in Paris, then went to England where he founded the Hallé Orchestra. He was married to Wilma Neruda. (Photo: Elliott & Fry, London) 100. BORIS HAMBOURG (1884–1954), Russian cellist. Studied with Becker. He later settled in Toronto where, with his brother Jan and his father Michael, he established the Hambourg Conservatory. (Photo: Foulsham & Banfield) 101. JAN HAMBOURG (1882–1947), Russian violinist. He studied with Wilhelmj, Ševčík and Ysaÿe, and toured extensively with his brothers Boris and Mark. (Photo: Foulsham & Banfield; signed 1908) 102. MARK HAMBOURG (1879–1960), Russian pianist. Student of Leschetizky; brother of Boris and Jan; his career began as a prodigy in 1888 and led to tours all over the world. 103. MARIE HALL (1884–1956), English violinist. She was a protégée of Elgar, who sent her to Wilhelmj for study. After further study with Ševčík, she became the premier female violinist of her time. (Photo: Barnes, Montreal)

Clara Haskil

104

105

May Harrison

106

107

104. CLARA HASKIL (1895–1960), Rumanian pianist. She appeared in Vienna at age seven, then studied with Fauré, Cortot and Busoni. She was noted for her Beethoven and her Mozart. (Photo: Emile Gos, Lausanne) 105. MISKA HAUSER (1822–1887), Slovakian violinist. A student of Kreutzer, he had sensational success as a child violinist. He later toured Australia and America. (Photo: J. Albert, Munich) 106. MAY HARRISON (1891–1959), English violinist. Student of Auer. She toured with her sisters Beatrice (a cellist) and Margaret (a pianist). (Photo: C. Vandyk, London) 107. OTTO HEGNER (1876–1907), Swiss pianist. As a child prodigy, he was brought over to America in 1888 as a rival to Hofmann, but although he was possibly superior, he did not attract much attention. (Photo: Napoleon Sarony, N.Y., 1889; signed 1889)

108

109

110

108. ADOLPH VON HENSELT (1814–1889), German pianist and composer. One of the great Romantic virtuosos, Henselt was very influential in Russia, where he spent forty years. His compositions have been revived recently. (Photo: William Klauser, N.Y.) 109. HENRI HERZ (1803–1888), Austrian pianist. Ranked with Moscheles and Johann Baptist Cramer as one of the premier pianists of his day, he toured Europe, the U. S., Mexico and the West Indies. (Photo: Gaston, Mathieu & Cie, Paris) 110. FERDINAND HILLER (1811–1885), German pianist, conductor and composer. A pupil of Aloys Schmitt, he appeared in public at age ten. He later studied with Hummel. His compositions are being revived. (Photo: Fritz Luckhardt, Vienna) 111. JASCHA HEIFETZ (born 1901), Russian-American violinist. Student of Auer. Both as a child prodigy and as a mature performer, Heifetz has been considered a unique phenomenon in the twentieth century, as Paganini was in the nineteenth, for perfection of style, tone and virtuosity. (Photo: Arnold Genthe, N.Y.)

112

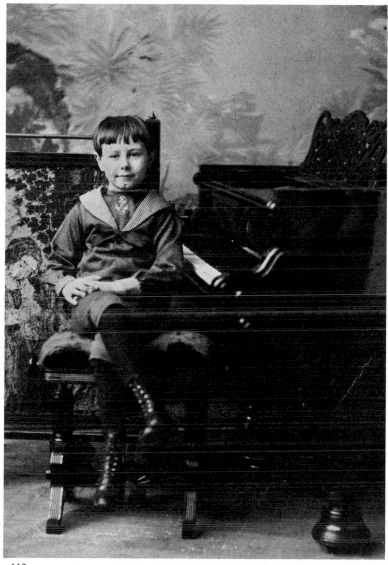

113

114

112. DAME MYRA HESS (1890–1965), English pianist. Her tours on the Continent and in America in the classical repertoire were always eagerly awaited. 113 & 114. JOSEF HOFMANN (1876–1957), Polish pianist active in America. As one of the most celebrated child prodigies in music history, Hofmann had a sensational American tour in 1887. He studied with Moszkowski and Anton Rubinstein (as the latter's only private pupil). As a mature virtuoso, he was considered the finest pianist of his time, with unrivaled tone and technique. He was associated with the Curtis Institute from its founding in 1924. See also photo 225. (Photo 113: Napoleon Sarony, N.Y., 1887. Photo 114: Gessford, N.Y.; signed 1905)

115

116

117

Souvenir from

Mieczysław Horszowski Nov. 1922

118

119

115. GUSTAV HOLLÄNDER (1885–1915), German violinist. Studied with Ferdinand David and Joachim. He began his career at age twenty and later appeared in chamber recitals with Grünfeld and Scharwenka. (Photo: Albert Meyer Nachf. Oscar Brettschneider) 116. JOSEPH HOLLMANN (1852–1927), Dutch cellist active in France. Student of Servais. Hollmann was very popular in Europe and America. Saint-Saëns wrote his second cello concerto for him. (Photo: Paul Berger, Paris) 117. JENÖ HUBAY (1858–1937), Hungarian violinist and composer. Student of Joachim and Vieuxtemps. Founder of the famous Hubay String Quartet in Budapest, he was celebrated as a virtuoso and a teacher. His pupils included Szigeti and Vecsey. 118. MIECZYSLAW HORSZOWSKI (born 1892), Polish pianist. A student of Leschetizky, he made his first public appearance at age nine. He was often associated with Casals, with whom he gave concerts and chamber recitals. (Photo: Mallais du Carroy; signed 1922) 119. VLADIMIR HOROWITZ (born 1904), Russian pianist active in America. One of the most celebrated virtuosos of the century. (Photo: Nickolas Muray)

120

121

122

123

120. BRONISLAW HUBERMAN (1882–1947), Polish violinist. Pupil of Joachim. In 1896 he played the Brahms violin concerto in Vienna to the warm approval of the composer. In 1936 he founded the Palestine (later Israel) Philharmonic. (Photo signed 1930) 121. ERNEST HUTCHESON (1871–1951), Australian pianist active in America. Student of Reinecke. Also respected as dean (1924–37) and then president of the Juilliard School. See also photo 143. (Photo: Thomas Coke Knight, N.Y., 1925) 122. FERDINAND HUMMEL (1855–1928), German composer and harpist. He gave concerts as a child harpist in 1864–67. (Photo: E. Bieber, Berlin; signed 1909) 123. HUNGARIAN QUARTET. Famous quartet founded in 1935 in Budapest. The members shown here are Zoltán Székely (1st violin), Alexander Moskowsky (2nd violin), Koromzay (viola) and Palotai (cello).

124

125

124. EUGENE ISTOMIN (born 1925), American pianist. Student of Serkin; known for his trio playing with Stern and Rose. Shown here (left) with Lillian Kallir (born 1937), an American pianist born in Prague of Austrian parentage, and her husband Claude Frank (born 1925), an American pianist who studied with Schnabel. 125. JOSÉ ITURBI (born 1895), Spanish pianist. This very popular performer made his American debut in 1928. (Photo signed 1936) 126. ANTONIO JANIGRO (born 1918), Italian cellist. His tours have included Europe, South America and Africa.

127

128

129

130

127 & 129. JOSEPH JOACHIM (1831–1907), German violinist. Student of Ferdinand David. His nobility of style made him one of the most venerated musicians in history and an institution in Berlin as a teacher. (Photo 127: Underwood & Underwood. Photo 129: Ernst Milster, Berlin) 128. JOACHIM QUARTET. Founded in 1869 by Joachim (1st violin), the quartet was one of the most celebrated of the nineteenth century. Shown with Joachim are Robert Hausmann (1852–1909, cello), Emanuel Wirth (viola, see photo 266) and Carl Halir (2nd violin, see photo 97). 130. RAFAEL JOSEFFY (1852–1915), Hungarian pianist. A student of Tausig, he settled in America, where he was a celebrated virtuoso and teacher. (Photo: Aimé Dupont, N.Y.; signed North Tarrytown, 1900)

131

131. WILLIAM KAPELL (1922–1953), American pianist. Student of Samaroff. His tragic death in an airplane crash robbed America of its most promising pianist. 132. EILEEN JOYCE (born ca. 1915), Australian pianist born in Tasmania. A student of Schnabel (in Germany), with a specialty in concertos, she has also done important film work (soundtracks and actual appearances).

BLÜTHNER

133

134

135

133. WILHELM KEMPFF (born 1895), German pianist. Highly regarded as a master pianist, especially in Beethoven. (Photo: Rudolf Betz, Munich) 134. EDWARD KILENYI, JR. (born 1911), American pianist. Student of Dohnányi. His career has included European tours. (Photo: James Abresch, N.Y.) 135. WILLIAM KINCAID (1896–1967), American flute virtuoso. As the great flutist in the Philadelphia Orchestra and as a teacher at the Curtis Institute, Kincaid helped establish an American tradition for excellence on that instrument. (Photo: Adrian Siegel) 136. HANS KINDLER (1892–1949), Dutch cellist active in America. After six years as first cellist of the Philadelphia Orchestra he had a concert career in the U. S. (Photo: Underwood & Underwood, 1926)

136

137

138

139

140

J. KOCIAN

141

137. RALPH KIRKPATRICK (born 1911), American harpsichordist. A student of Boulanger and Landowska, he has achieved international fame, particularly as a Bach specialist. 138. KARL KLINDWORTH (1830–1916), German pianist. Student of Liszt. Very popular as a pianist and teacher, he founded a famed music school in Berlin with Scharwenka. Shown with him here is Frederick Dawson (1868–1940), a British pianist who studied with Klindworth as well as with Hallé and Anton Rubinstein. 139. FRANZ KNEISEL (1865–1926), German violinist born in Bucharest. In 1885 he became concertmaster of the Boston Symphony and often appeared as a soloist. With his Kneisel Quartet he gave the American premieres of Beethoven's last quartets. (Photo: Bushnell, San Francisco; inscribed to Moritz Rosenthal, Salt Lake City, 1899) 140. PAUL KOCHANSKI (1887–1934), Polish violinist. Pupil of César Thomson. He specialized in modern music, especially that of his friend Szymanowski. (Photo signed 1918) 141. JAROSLAV KOCIAN (1883–1950), Czech violinist. Student of Ševčík and Dvořák. His success as a virtuoso was almost as great as that of his compatriot Kubelík.

143

144

142–144. FRITZ KREISLER (1875–1962), Austrian violinist and composer. Student of Auer. His concerts were received with enormous enthusiasm, and his following and popularity were very great. He became an American citizen in 1940, but even earlier he was an American institution. In photo 143 he is seen with George Barrère (see photo 13) and Ernest Hutcheson (see photo 121). In photo 144 he is seen with Georges Enesco (see photo 64) and Zino Francescatti (see photo 74). (Photo 142: Brown Bros. Photo 143: Herald Tribune, Fine, 1940)

145

145. SERGE KOUSSEVITZKY (1874–1951), Russian conductor and double-bass virtuoso. As the most celebrated performer on his instrument since Bottesini, he made a sensation at his Berlin concert in 1903. Because of the limited repertory for double bass, Koussevitzky devoted more time to conducting, becoming eminent especially as conductor of the Boston Symphony (1924–49). 146. JAN KUBELÍK (1880–1940), Czech violinist. Student of Ševčík. Enormously popular, Kubelík was considered one of the outstanding violinists of the day. (Photo: Tupper, Cambridge; signed 1907) 147. FRIEDA KWAST-HODDAP (1880–1949), German pianist. A student of Busoni, she was regarded by Grainger as the finest woman pianist he ever encountered. (Photo: Dührkoop, 1909) 148. FREDERIC LAMOND (1868–1948), Scottish pianist. Student of von Bülow, Clara Schumann and Liszt. Especially noted for his playing of Beethoven. 149. EMIL KRONKE (1865–1938), German pianist. Student of Reinecke. Composed several virtuoso pieces for piano. (Photo: Hahn Nachflg., Dresden, 1906; signed Dresden, 1909)

146

147

148

149

150

151

152

153

150 & 151. WANDA LANDOWSKA (1877–1959), Polish harpsichordist and pianist. Student of Moszkowski. As the principal in the harpsichord revival and an authority on old music, she was one of the great musicians of the twentieth century and unrivaled in her playing of Bach and Mozart. In photo 151 she is seen playing for Tolstoy at his home in 1909. (Photo 151 signed 1921) 152. ALICIA DE LARROCHA (born 1923), Spanish pianist. Student of Frank Marshall (shown with her). One of the leading female pianists of the day, she began to make public appearances at age five. 153. FERDINAND LAUB (1832–1875), Czech violinist and composer. He enjoyed an international career. (Photo: Heinrich Graf, Berlin) 154. ETHEL LEGINSKA (actually Liggins, 1886–1970), English pianist. Student of Leschetizky. Popular in the U. S. and Europe, she was known as "the disappearing pianist" because of her frequent cancellations.

154

155

156

155 & 156. MISCHA LEVITZKI (1898–1941), Russian-American pianist. A student of Dohnányi, Levitzki had a brilliant career as a virtuoso. (Photo 155: Ortho, N.Y.; signed 1929) 157. JOSEF LHÉVINNE (1874–1944), Russian pianist. Student of Safonov. Unrivaled as an interpreter of the Romantic composers, especially Chopin. (Photo: I. E. Hori) 158. ROSINA LHÉVINNE (born 1880), Russian pianist active in America. A fine virtuoso, she was even more renowned as a pedagogue, teaching both privately and at the Juilliard Graduate School. She is seen here with her husband Josef. (Photo: Cohope) 159. THEODOR LESCHETIZKY (1830–1915), Polish pianist. A virtuosic pupil of Czerny, he was a great teacher whose pupils included Paderewski, Schnabel and Gabrilovitch.

157

159

158

161

162

160. FRANZ (FERENC) LISZT (1811–1886), Hungarian
pianist and composer. The most legendary piano virtuoso
in history, his compositions are landmarks of pianism and
Romanticism. Also famed as a teacher, with such pupils as
Tausig, Menter, von Bülow and Rosenthal. 161. EUGENE
LIST (born 1918), American pianist. Student of Samaroff.
He made his debut in 1935 and has had an international
reputation ever since. (Photo signed Quebec, 1941)
162. DINU LIPATTI (1917–1950), Rumanian pianist.
Student of Cortot. The death of Lipatti at thirty-three
robbed the world of one of the greatest musical talents of
the century.

To Martha B. Saunders, grateful and [...]
membrance of my association [...] Institute [...]
Institute of Music.

Arthur [...]

163

Dec. 1945.

Pour notre
charmante amie,
Thérèse Galipeauet, avec
vos souvenirs bien sympath[...]
et à l'espoir de la revoir [...]
Bien sincère [...]

Felix [...]

Pierre [...]

164

165

163. ARTHUR LOESSER (1894–1969), American pianist. This well-known virtuoso began a long tenure at the Cleveland Institute of Music in 1926. (Photo signed Cleveland, 1932) 164. LUBOSHUTZ AND NEMENOFF. The most celebrated duo pianists of the century were Pierre Luboshutz (1894–1971), Russian-American, and his wife Genia Nemenoff (born 1908), French. (Photo signed 1945) 165. MARGUERITE LONG (1878–1966), French pianist. Especially famed as an interpreter of Debussy and Ravel; the latter dedicated his Piano Concerto in G to her. (Photo: Paris Match)

166

Sofie Menter

167

168

166. NATHAN MILSTEIN (born 1904), Russian violinist. Student of Auer. With his first appearance in the U. S. in 1928, he established himself as a virtuoso. (Photo signed 1936) 167. SOPHIE MENTER (1846–1918), German pianist. Liszt's favorite pupil, she enjoyed a great reputation. She was married to the cellist David Popper. 168. HENRI MARTEAU (1874–1934), French violinist. This outstanding virtuoso eventually succeeded Joachim at the Hochschule für Musik in Berlin. He became a Swedish citizen in 1920. (Photo: Aimé Dupont, N.Y.)

169

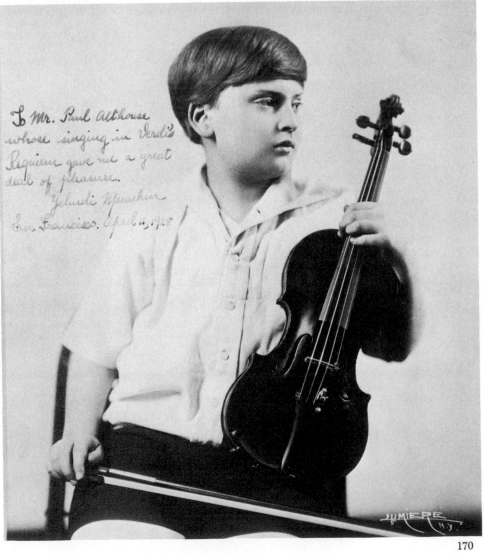

170

71

169. MISCHA MISCHAKOV (born 1895), Russian violinist. Student of Auer. A legendary virtuoso, he was contented with being the crack concertmaster of America's great orchestras, including the NBC Symphony with Toscanini from 1937. (Photo: Detroit Symphony)

170 & 171. YEHUDI MENUHIN (born 1916), American violinist. One of the most celebrated child prodigies to play the violin, he has also had a fine career as a mature artist. (Photo 170: Lumière, N.Y.; inscribed to the tenor Paul Althouse, 1928. Photo 171 signed 1946)

172

173

174

175

172. IGNAZ MOSCHELES (1794–1870), Czech pianist and composer. A pianist of the first magnitude, Moscheles had close associations with Beethoven and Mendelssohn. (Photo: August Brasch, Leipzig) 173 & 174. BENNO MOISEIWITSCH (1890–1963), Russian pianist active in England. He toured all over the world, becoming especially noted in the Romantic repertoire. (Photo 173 signed 1935. Photo 174 signed 1948) 175 & 176. ERICA MORINI (born 1904), Austrian violinist active in America. A student of Ševčík, she was one of the most celebrated female violinists of her day. (Photo 176: Albert Petersen, 1930; inscribed to Josef Hofmann, 1930)

176

177

178

177 & 178. MORITZ MOSZKOWSKI (1854–1925), Polish-German pianist and composer active in France. Renowned as a pianist, he was well known for his Spanish-style compositions. (Photo 178: Gerschel, Paris) 179. TIVADAR NACHEZ (1859–1930), Hungarian violinist. A student of Joachim, he had an international career as a virtuoso. 180. WILMA NERUDA (LADY HALLÉ, 1839–1911), Czech violinist active in Britain. Considered the peer of any of her contemporaries, she married Charles Hallé in 1888. (Photo: Bassano)

179

180

181

182

94

183

181. GINETTE NEVEU (1919–1949), French violinist. A pupil of Flesch, she was considered the outstanding female violinist of her time when she died in an airplane crash. (Photo signed 1949) 182. ELLY NEY (1882–1968), German pianist. Student of Leschetizky and Sauer; she had an international career. 183. GUIOMAR NOVAËS (1895–1979), Brazilian pianist. From the beginning of her career as a prodigy, she was considered a sensitive pianist and a performer of the highest calibre.

184

184. DAVID OISTRAKH (1908–1974), Russian violinist. The most eminent violinist in the Soviet Union, he has enjoyed an international reputation since 1937, when he won the international competition in Brussels. 185. FRANZ ONDŘÍČEK (1859–1922), Czech violinist. His tours took him to America, Siberia and the Far East. 186. FERNAND OUBRADOUS (born 1903), French bassoonist. The most remarkable bassoonist of his time, Oubradous has done extensive reconstructions of old French music. 187. ERWIN NYIREGYHÁZI (born 1903), Hungarian pianist active in America. Student of Dohnányi. The most celebrated child prodigy since Mozart, he enjoyed a fine career but disappeared in the 1930s only to be rediscovered in the 1970s in straitened circumstances. His subsequent recordings caused a sensation, and he is now considered by many authorities as one of the most important living pianists.

185

187

Avec mes compliment pour
l'action do Monsieur James Conner.
H. Dubredous

186

97

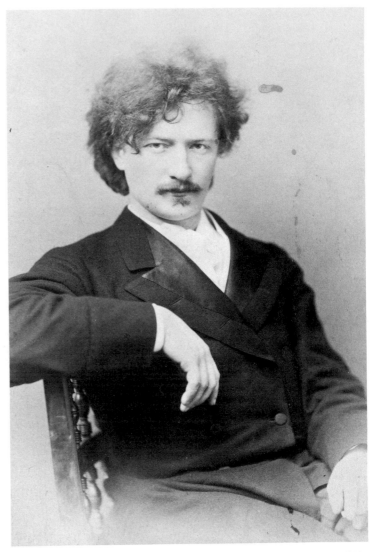

188

189

188. VLADIMIR DE PACHMANN (1848–1933), Russian pianist. De Pachmann had an extraordinary reputation as an interpreter of Chopin. 189 & 190. IGNACE JAN PADEREWSKI (1860–1941), Polish pianist. As the most celebrated pianist to appear after Liszt, he was a Polish institution and became president of Poland in Exile in 1940. (Photo 189: W. Kurtz, N.Y.)

191

Ernst Pauer
Pianist

192

193

194

195

191. KARL PEMBAUR (1876–1939), Austrian organist active in Germany. Student of Rheinberger. (Photo signed 1909) 192. ERNST PAUER (1826–1905), Austrian pianist. A student of Mozart's son W. A. Mozart, Jr., Pauer had a reputation in London and in Austria, where he became court pianist in 1866. (Photo: H. Hering, London) 193. ALEXANDER PETCHNIKOV (1873–1949), Russian violinist. Toured internationally. 194. WALTER PETZET (1866–1941), German pianist. Student of Rheinberger; active mostly in Dresden as a teacher and composer. 195. EGON PETRI (1881–1962), German pianist. Pupil of Busoni and Carreño. He enjoyed a successful international career as performer and teacher. (Photo: Blanche de Lorière, N.Y.; signed Boston, 1934)

196. ISIDOR PHILIPP (1863–1958), French pianist. A student of Saint-Saëns, he was one of the most celebrated pianists of the first half of this century. (Photo signed 1942) 197. ALFREDO PIATTI (1822–1901), Italian cellist. The most distinguished cellist of his day, with a reputation cor-responding to that of the violinist Joachim. (Photo: H. Prothmann, Königsberg) 198. GREGOR PIATIGORSKY (born 1903), Russian cellist. Piatigorsky is greatly esteemed and many cello concertos have been written for him, including one by Hindemith. (Photo signed 193?)

198

199

200

201

202

203

199. VÁŠA PŘÍHODA (born 1900), Czech violinist. He made his U. S. debut in 1921. (Photo ca. 1929) 200. LOUIS PLAIDY (1810–1874), German violinist and pianist. He began professionally as a violinist, but became such a fine pianist that Mendelssohn engaged him as piano professor at the Leipzig Conservatory. (Photo: August Brasch, Leipzig) 201. DAVID POPPER (1843–1913), Czech cellist. As first cellist of the Vienna Court Orchestra from 1868 to 1873, Popper was one of the celebrated cellists of his time. He was married to Sophie Menter.

(Photo: August Brasch, Leipzig) 202. ROBERT POLLAK (1880–1962), Austrian violinist active in America. He became a professor of violin at the Los Angeles Conservatory. (Photo: A. de Lalancy, Geneva; signed Geneva, 1909) 203. FRANCIS PLANTÉ (1839–1934), French pianist. The legendary pianist retired about 1900, vowing "never to be seen again in public." He reappeared in 1915 but was hidden from the audience by a screen. (Photo: Benque & Co., Paris)

205

204. WILLIAM PRIMROSE (born 1903), Scottish violist active in America. Studied with Ysaÿe. In 1937 he became first violist of the NBC Symphony under Toscanini and was perhaps the premier resident violist in the U.S. 205. MICHAEL RABIN (1936–1970), American violinist. He is seen here with pianist Donald Voorhees. (Photo: NBC Radio, 1955) 206. RAOUL PUGNO (1852–1914), French pianist. Pugno gave celebrated recitals with Ysaÿe. He was an early champion of the works of Franck. (Photo: Herschel)

206

207

208

207. EDUARD REMÉNYI (1830–1898), Hungarian violinist. He toured worldwide. (Photo: Sarony, N.Y.; signed N.Y., 1878) 208. MAX REGER (1873–1916), German composer and pianist. The celebrated composer toured as a pianist in 1901–04. 209. SERGE RACHMANINOFF (1873–1943), Russian pianist and composer.

Popular as a composer, Rachmaninoff was one of the greatest pianists of his time and a virtuoso of staggering abilities, as his compositions (written for himself) demonstrate. 210. CARL REINECKE (1824–1910), German pianist and composer. His Romantic compositions are still performed. (Photo: August Brasch, Leipzig)

209

210

212

211. FLORIZEL VON REUTER (born 1890), American violinist. Student of Thomson and Sauret. Toured successfully and settled in Munich. 212. RUGGIERO RICCI (born 1920), American violinist. He gave his first performance at age eight; equally successful as a mature virtuoso. 213. SVIATOSLAV RICHTER (born 1914), Russian pianist. He has been a renowned virtuoso from the time of his prizewinning appearance in 1945, and has made tours in the West. (Photo: Clive Barda, London)

211

214

215

214. EDOUARD RISLER (1873–1929), German pianist active in France. Student of Diémer, Klindworth, Stavenhagen and d'Albert. He specialized in complete cycles of Beethoven, Bach and Chopin. 215. LEONARD ROSE (born 1918), American cellist. This outstanding member of the NBC Symphony under Toscanini later became celebrated as a virtuoso and in a trio with Isaac Stern and Eugene Istomin. (Photo: Bruno of Hollywood, N.Y.) 216. JULIE RIVÉ-KING (1857–1937), American pianist. Student of Reinecke and Liszt. Her American debut was with the N.Y. Philharmonic in 1875. She enjoyed a long and distinguished career. (Photo: Joseph Gray Kitchell; signed 1897) 217. MORIZ ROSENTHAL (1862–1946), Polish pianist. One of Liszt's most celebrated pupils, he is considered one of the greatest virtuosos in pianistic history. (Photo: Aimé Dupont, N.Y.)

216

218

219

218. ANTON RUBINSTEIN (1829–1894), Russian pianist and composer. As a pianist Rubinstein had a reputation second only to his great contemporary Liszt. (Photo: Gurney & Son, N.Y.) 219 & 220. MSTISLAV ROSTROPO-

VITCH (born 1927), Russian cellist. Famed since his prize-winning performance in 1950 at the Prague Festival, he left Russia in the late 1960s with his wife, soprano Galina Vishnevskaya. (Photo: Clive Barda, London)

du Bois
Toronto.

221

116

222

223

224

221. ARTHUR RUBINSTEIN (born 1886), Polish pianist active in America. Student of Barth. He is noted for his Chopin. (Photo: Charles du Bois, Toronto; signed Quebec, 1944) 222. CAMILLE SAINT-SAËNS (1835–1921), French composer, pianist and organist. The composer had a great reputation as an organ and piano virtuoso. He is shown here with French conductor Pierre Monteux. (Photo: M. Rol, Paris) 223. PROSPER SAINTON (1813–1890), French violinist. Student of Habeneck. Especially popular in England, he was concertmaster of the London Philharmonic from 1846 to 1854. (Photo: W. & D. Downey, Newcastle & London) 224. VASSILY SAFONOV (1852–1918), Russian pianist and conductor. He made his pianistic debut in St. Petersburg in 1880. His fame as a conductor was even greater. (Photo signed 1909)

225

226

227

228

225. DAVID SAPERTON (1889–1970), American pianist. An astounding virtuoso and one of the very few who could play Godowsky's piano music without difficulty, he married Godowsky's daughter Vanita. In this picture Saperton is at the left; with him is Josef Hofmann (see photos 113 & 114). 226. PABLO DE SARASATE (1844–1908), Spanish violinist and composer. A nineteenth-century virtuoso of great fame and popularity whose compositions are still performed. 227. OLGA SAMAROFF (1882–1948), American pianist. Student of Ernest Hutcheson. Married to Stokowski (1911–23), the brilliant Samaroff was also an influential educator. (Photo: Kubey-Rembrandt Studios, Philadelphia; signed 1925) 228. JESÚS MARÍA SANROMÁ (born 1903), Puerto Rican pianist. Student of Cortot and Schnabel. Especially noted for his championship of modern music. (Photo signed Boston, 1933)

Copyright 1899
by B. J. Falk

Emil Sauer.

229

229. EMIL VON SAUER (1862–1942), German pianist. Student of Nicholas Rubinstein and Liszt. Considered one of the last of the Romantic pianists. (Photo: B. J. Falk, N.Y., 1899) 230. ELIE ROBERT SCHMITZ (1889–1949), French pianist. Student of Diémer. He first toured as an accompanist to primadonnas (such as Emma Eames), and later organized the Association des Concerts Schmitz in Paris and the Pro Musica in N.Y. 231. XAVER SCHAR-WENKA (1850–1924), German pianist and composer. A student of Kullak, he was a Romantic pianist and composer who toured worldwide. 232. EMILE SAURET (1852–1920), French violinist. Student of Vieuxtemps and Bériot. Famed as a child prodigy and later as an exponent of the French school. He was married to Teresa Carreño. (Photo: Wilhelm Fechner, Berlin)

230

231

232

233

233. WOLFGANG SCHNEIDERHAN (born 1915), Austrian violinist. A student of Ševčík and a child prodigy, he became concertmaster of the Vienna Philharmonic in 1932. He is seen here with his wife, soprano Irmgard Seefried. 234. ARTUR SCHNABEL (1882–1951), Austrian pianist active in Germany, Switzerland and the U. S. Student of Leschetizky. A pianist of enormous influence, he established a new German style, more cerebral and less Romantic. The most celebrated pianist of his time—more for his musicianship than his virtuosity—he was most closely associated with Beethoven, although considered superb in Schubert and Mozart. (Photo: Willinger) 235. HENRY SCHRADIEK (1846–1918), German violinist. Student of Ferdinand David. After tenure as concertmaster of the Leipzig Gewandhaus Orchestra, 1874–83, he moved to New York, where he was active as a teacher and conductor.

235

234

236

237

236. KARL SCHRÖDER (1848–1935), German cellist. Soloist with the Leipzig Gewandhaus Orchestra, 1874–81, he was also a successful composer. (Photo: Atelier Perscheid, Leipzig) 237. CLARA SCHUMANN (née Wieck, 1819–1896), German pianist and composer. The most celebrated woman instrumentalist of the nineteenth century, she was especially famed for her playing of her husband Robert Schumann's music as well as that of her close friend Brahms. (Photo: Carl von Jagemann, Vienna) 238. ALBERT SCHWEITZER (1875–1965), German (Alsatian) physician and organist. Student of Widor. Most noted for his performances of Bach, whose organ music he restored to popularity.

239

240. ANDRÉS SEGOVIA (born 1893), Spanish guitarist.
The most celebrated classical guitar virtuoso of modern
times. 240. TOSCHA SEIDEL (1899–1962), Russian violinist. Student of Auer. Many worldwide tours established
his skill. (Photo: Blackstone Studios; signed 1938)
241. RUDOLF SERKIN (born 1903), Bohemian pianist active in America. One of the finest pianists of the modern
German tradition, he made his American debut in 1933.
He succeeded Josef Hofmann as head of the piano depart-
ment at the Curtis Institute. (Photo signed 1937)

240

to Mrs. Galimir
with best wishes.

Rudolf Serkin

2. V. 1961

242

243

242. ALEXANDER SILOTI (1863–1945), Russian pianist. Student of Nicholas Rubinstein, Tchaikovsky and Liszt. Considered one of Liszt's finest pupils, Siloti made many tours of Europe and America. 243. FRANÇOIS SERVAIS (1807–1866), Belgian cellist. A concert in Paris in 1834 launched a brilliant career that took the cellist worldwide. (Photo: Géruzet Frères, Brussels) 244. HANS SITT (1850–

1922), Czech violinist. In the first Brodsky Quartet he played viola. (Photo signed 1909) 245. CAMILLO SIVORI (1815–1894), Italian violinist. He appeared in public at age six and impressed Paganini, who allegedly took him as his only pupil. His subsequent career and tours of North and South America and Europe established him as an astounding virtuoso. (Photo: F. Benque, Trieste)

244

245

246

247

248

246 & 247. ALBERT SPALDING (1888–1953), American violinist. He made his debut in Paris in 1905, and was known as the "blueblood violinist." (Photo 246: Dover Street Studios, London; signed 1911. Photo 247: signed 1942) 248. RUTH SLENCZYNSKA (born 1925), American pianist. A sensational child prodigy, she made her debut in Berlin at age six. Her transition to mature performer was difficult and she retired, resuming her career with success in 1954. (Photo: James J. Kriegsmann, N.Y.) 249. ISAAC STERN (born 1920), Russian-American violinist. He made his debut in San Francisco at age eleven. Among the most distinguished violinists of his time, he forms a famous trio with pianist Eugene Istomin and cellist Leonard Rose. (Photo signed 1954)

249

250

251

250. BERNHARD STAVENHAGEN (1862–1914), German pianist. Student of Kiel and Liszt (one of the last, 1885–86). He toured the U. S. and Europe, then devoted himself to conducting and composing. (Photo: A. de Lalancy, Geneva; signed 1909) 251. TOSSY SPIVAKOVSKY (born 1907), Russian violinist active in America. He studied with Willy Hess in Berlin, where he made his debut at age ten. He toured Europe, Australia and then the U. S., where he established himself as an outstanding virtuoso. 252. JANOS STARKER (born 1924), Hungarian cellist. One of the outstanding postwar cellists. (Photo: Angus McBean, London)

253

253. JOSEPH SZIGETI (1892–1973), Hungarian violinist. Student of Hubay; debut in 1905. Highly regarded as an interpreter, Szigeti also championed new music; for example, he performed the world premiere of Bloch's violin concerto in 1938. (Photo signed 1942) 254. EMIL TELMÁNYI (born 1892), Hungarian violinist. Student of Hubay; resident in Denmark from 1919. He made a successful U. S. tour in 1950. (Photo: Lisi Jessen) 255. JACQUES THIBAUD (1880–1953), French violinist. He formed a legendary trio with Alfred Cortot and Pablo Casals (see photo 46). (Photo signed Quebec, 1947) 256. LIONEL TERTIS (born 1876), English violist. A student of the Leipzig Conservatory. (Photo signed 1936) 257. CARL TAUSIG (1841–1871), German pianist born in Warsaw. A pupil of Thalberg and Liszt, he was considered the near equal of the latter as a virtuoso. (Photo: W. Klauser, N.Y.)

254

255

256

257

259

260

258. DIMITRI TIOMKIN (1894–1979), Russian composer and pianist active in America. He is seen here standing beside GEORGE GERSHWIN (1898–1937), American pianist and composer. Tiomkin was renowned as a pianist, especially in Europe, where he gave the European premiere of Gershwin's *Rhapsody in Blue*. Gershwin himself gave the world premiere in New York. (Photo: G.-L.

Manuel Frères, Paris) 259. ROSALYN TURECK (born 1914), American pianist. A student of Samaroff, she made her debut at age eleven and has emerged as a Bach specialist. 260. CAMILLA URSO (1842–1902), French violinist. She was especially noted for her American tours with the opera stars Marietta Alboni and Henriette Sontag in the 1850s. (Photo: Sarony, N.Y.)

261

262

261. ALEXANDER UNINSKY (born 1910), Russian pianist. Since 1939 he has toured all over the world. In 1955 he joined the Toronto Conservatory. (Photo signed 1944) 262. ADELA VERNE (1877–1952), English pianist. A student of Paderewski and member of a famed musical family, she was popular in England and America. 263. HENRI VIEUXTEMPS (1820–1881), Belgian violinist and composer. After Bériot, with whom he studied, he was the most celebrated exponent of the French school. The pieces he wrote for himself give evidence of his virtuosity. 264. FRANZ VON VECSEY (1893–1935), Hungarian violinist. Pupil of Hubay; tours established his reputation as a prodigy in 1903–1905.

263

264

139

265

Professor Emanuel Wirth

266

267

268

265. HENRI WIENIAWSKI (1835–1880), Polish violinist. One of the great violinists of his time, he wrote numerous works that are still performed. (Photo: Sarony, N.Y.)
266. EMANUEL WIRTH (1842–1923), Bohemian violinist and violist. A member of the Joachim Quartet (see photo 128), he later founded his own trio with cellist Robert Hausmann and pianist Heinrich Barth. (Photo: Albert Meyer Nachf. Oscar Brettschneider; signed 1909)

267. AUGUST WILHELMJ (1845–1908), German violinist. A pupil of Ferdinand David, his career took him all over the world. In 1876, he was concertmaster for the first complete *Ring* in Bayreuth. (Photo: August Linde, Gotha)
268. BRUNO WALTER (1876–1962), conductor and pianist. Student of Ehrlich. One of the master conductors, Walter often led concerts from the keyboard, especially in Mozart concertos. (Photo: Neofot, Berlin)

269

270

269. MICHAEL ZACHAREWITSCH (1879–1953), Russian violinist active in England. Student of Ševčík and Ysaÿe; protégé of Tchaikovsky. 270 & 271. EUGÈNE YSAÿE (1858–1931), Belgian violinist and composer. As a violinist, the major rival of Joachim. In photo 271 he is seen making an acoustic recording. (Photo 270: J. Lacroix, Geneva. Photo 271: Underwood & Underwood)

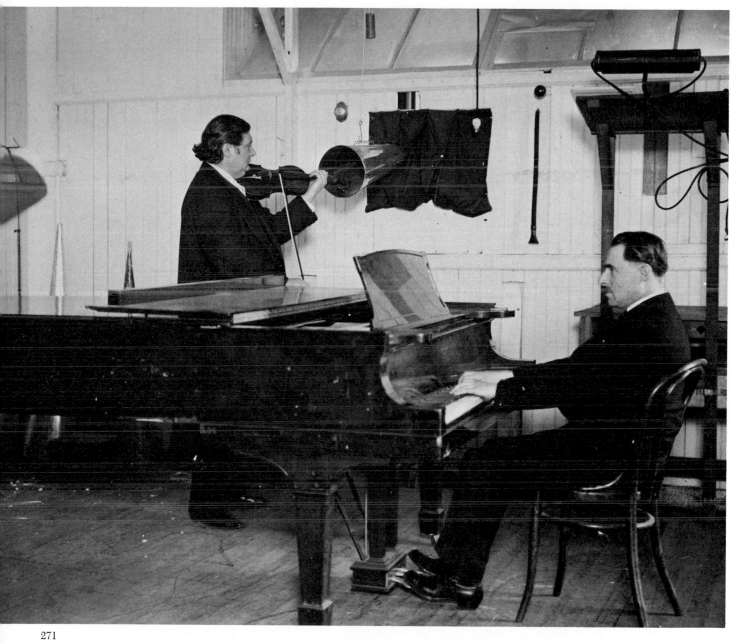

271

273

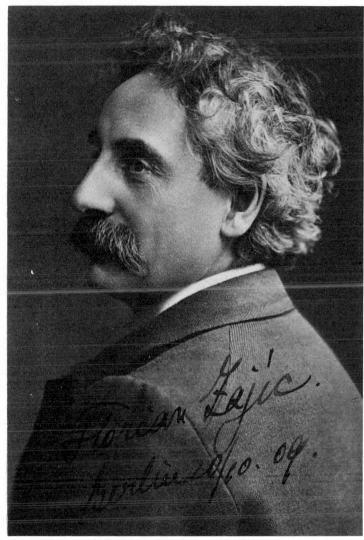

274

272 & 273. EFREM ZIMBALIST (born 1889), Russian violinist active in America. Student of Auer. From his debut in 1907, Zimbalist was regarded as an eminent violinist. (Photo 272: Hänse-Herrmann. Photo 273 signed 1929) 274. FLORIAN ZAJIC (1853–1926), Bohemian violinist and composer. He was a theater violinist and a teacher at the Stern Conservatory in Berlin, and also gave sonata recitals. (Photo: E. Bieber, Berlin; signed 1909)

INDEX

The performers are listed by their instruments. Surnames beginning with
the elements d', de and von are listed under the element that follows these.
References are to figure numbers rather than page numbers.